BE
UNIQUE

BE UNIQUE

A Journal for
Self-Awareness and Self-Acceptance

Monica Moore, MD

purposely
created
PUBLISHING

BE UNIQUE: A JOURNAL FOR SELF-AWARENESS
AND SELF-ACCEPTANCE
Published by Purposely Created Publishing Group™
Copyright © 2020 Monica Moore, MD
All rights reserved.

Printed in the United States of America

ISBN: 2-236-64484-1-978

Special discounts are available on bulk quantity purchases by book clubs, associations and special interest groups. For details email: sales@publishyourgift.com or call (6228-949 (888. For information log on to www.PublishYourGift.com

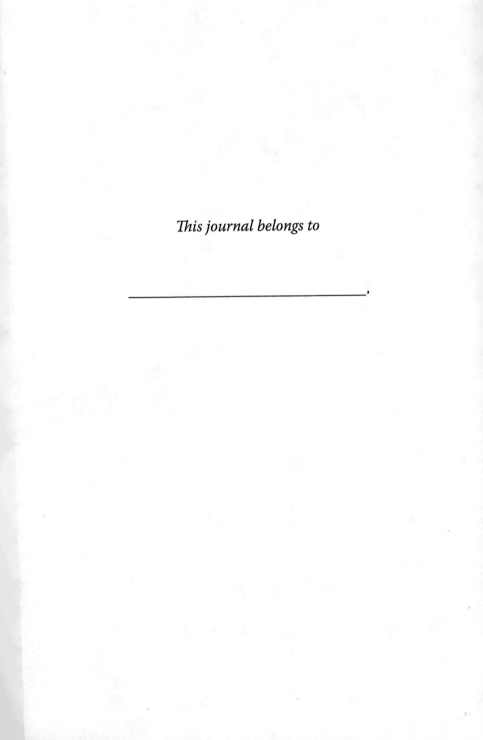

This journal belongs to

_____.

This journal is dedicated to all the brave and confident girls.

HOW TO USE THIS JOURNAL

∞

I designed this journal as a guide for you on your journey to self-acceptance. My goal is that this will help you make a daily effort to recognize your self-worth, importance, and value to the world.

I want you to start and end each day by writing in your journal. You will start by making an affirmation.

An affirmation is a positive statement that defines who you are and helps you to overcome negative thoughts about yourself. When written and stated often, affirmations can help you change the way you think about yourself.

Repeat this affirmation to yourself all day, especially when someone or something tries to make you change how you feel about yourself. Own this affirmation.

Example: I am smart.

Next, I want you to write a declarative statement. In this declarative statement, you will state exactly what you will accomplish that day. Be intentional about what it is you will accomplish and do everything in your power to make it happen.

Again, repeat this statement to yourself as encouragement to accomplish the goal you set for yourself.

Example: I will pass my test today.

You will end each night celebrating something you accomplished. Consider it a #WIN for the day. When we celebrate our wins, we acknowledge that we accomplished a goal and give ourselves the praise we deserve for the accomplishment we achieved.

Example: I tried my best on my test today.

I hope that you find this journal helpful, as I thought of you when I designed it. I want you to succeed in every area of your life. I know you have what it takes. Now you have to believe it too. Go after your dreams with confidence.

One last thing! The title of the book was placed at the top of each page for you to color it in your own unique way!!!!

Day 1 _____ (date)

I am

_____

_____

Today, I will

_____

_____

Today, I

_____

_____

My overall thoughts about my day:

_____

_____

_____

_____

_____

Day 2 _____ (date)

I am

_____

_____

Today, I will

_____

_____

Today, I

_____

_____

My overall thoughts about my day:

_____

_____

_____

_____

_____

Day 3 _____ (date)

I am

_____

_____

Today, I will

_____

_____

Today, I

_____

_____

My overall thoughts about my day:

_____

_____

_____

_____

_____

Day 4 _____ (date)

I am

_____

_____

Today, I will

_____

_____

Today, I

_____

_____

My overall thoughts about my day:

_____

_____

_____

_____

_____

BE
UNIQUE

Day 3 _____ (date)

I am

_____

_____

Today, I will

_____

_____

Today, I

_____

_____

My overall thoughts about my day:

_____

_____

_____

_____

_____

Day 6 _____ (date)

I am

_____

_____

Today, I will

_____

_____

Today, I

_____

_____

My overall thoughts about my day:

_____

_____

_____

_____

_____

Day 7 _____ (date)

I am

_____

_____

Today, I will

_____

_____

Today, I

_____

_____

My overall thoughts about my day:

_____

_____

_____

_____

_____

Day 8 _____ (date)

I am

_____

_____

Today, I will

_____

_____

Today, I

_____

_____

My overall thoughts about my day:

_____

_____

_____

_____

_____

BE UNIQUE

Day 9 _____ (date)

I am

_____

_____

Today, I will

_____

_____

Today, I

_____

_____

My overall thoughts about my day:

_____

_____

_____

_____

_____

Day 10 _____ (date)

I am

_____

_____

Today, I will

_____

_____

Today, I

_____

_____

My overall thoughts about my day:

_____

_____

_____

_____

_____

Day 11 _____ (date)

I am

_____

_____

Today, I will

_____

_____

Today, I

_____

_____

My overall thoughts about my day:

_____

_____

_____

_____

_____

Day 12 _____ (date)

I am

_____

_____

Today, I will

_____

_____

Today, I

_____

_____

My overall thoughts about my day:

_____

_____

_____

_____

_____

Day 13 _____ (date)

I am

_____

_____

Today, I will

_____

_____

Today, I

_____

_____

My overall thoughts about my day:

_____

_____

_____

_____

_____

Day 14 _____ (date)

I am

_____

_____

Today, I will

_____

_____

Today, I

_____

_____

My overall thoughts about my day:

_____

_____

_____

_____

_____

Day 15 _____ (date)

I am

_____

_____

Today, I will

_____

_____

Today, I

_____

_____

My overall thoughts about my day:

_____

_____

_____

_____

_____

Day 16 _____ (date)

I am

_____

_____

Today, I will

_____

_____

Today, I

_____

_____

My overall thoughts about my day:

_____

_____

_____

_____

_____

BE UNIQUE

Day 17 _____ (date)

I am

_____

_____

Today, I will

_____

_____

Today, I

_____

_____

My overall thoughts about my day:

_____

_____

_____

_____

_____

Day 18 _____ (date)

I am

_____

_____

Today, I will

_____

_____

Today, I

_____

_____

My overall thoughts about my day:

_____

_____

_____

_____

_____

Day 19 _____ (date)

I am

_____

_____

Today, I will

_____

_____

Today, I

_____

_____

My overall thoughts about my day:

_____

_____

_____

_____

_____

Day 20 _____ (date)

I am

_____

_____

Today, I will

_____

_____

Today, I

_____

_____

My overall thoughts about my day:

_____

_____

_____

_____

_____

Day 21 _____ (date)

I am

_____

_____

Today, I will

_____

_____

Today, I

_____

_____

My overall thoughts about my day:

_____

_____

_____

_____

_____

Day 22 _____ (date)

I am

_____

_____

Today, I will

_____

_____

Today, I

_____

_____

My overall thoughts about my day:

_____

_____

_____

_____

_____

BE UNIQUE

Day 23 _____ (date)

I am

_____

_____

Today, I will

_____

_____

Today, I

_____

_____

My overall thoughts about my day:

_____

_____

_____

_____

_____

Day 24 _____ (date)

I am

_____

_____

Today, I will

_____

_____

Today, I

_____

_____

My overall thoughts about my day:

_____

_____

_____

_____

_____

BE
UNIQUE

Day 25 _____ (date)

I am

_____

_____

Today, I will

_____

_____

Today, I

_____

_____

My overall thoughts about my day:

_____

_____

_____

_____

_____

Day 26 _____ (date)

I am

_____

_____

Today, I will

_____

_____

Today, I

_____

_____

My overall thoughts about my day:

_____

_____

_____

_____

_____

BE UNIQUE

Day 27 _____._____ (date)

I am

_____

_____

Today, I will

_____

_____

Today, I

_____

_____

My overall thoughts about my day:

_____

_____

_____

_____

_____

Day 28 _____ (date)

I am

_____

_____

Today, I will

_____

_____

Today, I

_____

_____

My overall thoughts about my day:

_____

_____

_____

_____

_____

Day 29 _____ (date)

I am

_____

_____

Today, I will

_____

_____

Today, I

_____

_____

My overall thoughts about my day:

_____

_____

_____

_____

Day 30 _____ (date)

I am

_____

_____

Today, I will

_____

_____

Today, I

_____

_____

My overall thoughts about my day:

_____

_____

_____

_____

_____

Day 31 _____ (date)

I am

_____

_____

Today, I will

_____

_____

Today, I

_____

_____

My overall thoughts about my day:

_____

_____

_____

_____

_____

Day 32 _____ (date)

I am

_____

_____

Today, I will

_____

_____

Today, I

_____

_____

My overall thoughts about my day:

_____

_____

_____

_____

_____

Day 33 _____ (date)

I am

_____

_____

Today, I will

_____

_____

Today, I

_____

_____

My overall thoughts about my day:

_____

_____

_____

_____

_____

Day 34 _____ (date)

I am

_____

_____

Today, I will

_____

_____

Today, I

_____

_____

My overall thoughts about my day:

_____

_____

_____

_____

_____

Day 35 _____ (date)

I am

_____

_____

Today, I will

_____

_____

Today, I

_____

_____

My overall thoughts about my day:

_____

_____

_____

_____

_____

Day 36 _____ (date)

I am

_____

_____

Today, I will

_____

_____

Today, I

_____

_____

My overall thoughts about my day:

_____

_____

_____

_____

_____

Day 37 _____ (date)

I am

_____

_____

Today, I will

_____

_____

Today, I

_____

_____

My overall thoughts about my day:

_____

_____

_____

_____

_____

Day 38 _____ (date)

I am

_____

_____

Today, I will

_____

_____

Today, I

_____

_____

My overall thoughts about my day:

_____

_____

_____

_____

_____

BE UNIQUE

Day 39 _____ (date)

I am

_____

_____

Today, I will

_____

_____

Today, I

_____

_____

My overall thoughts about my day:

_____

_____

_____

_____

_____

Day 40 _____ (date)

I am

_____

_____

Today, I will

_____

_____

Today, I

_____

_____

My overall thoughts about my day:

_____

_____

_____

_____

_____

Day 41 _____ (date)

I am

_____

_____

Today, I will

_____

_____

Today, I

_____

_____

My overall thoughts about my day:

_____

_____

_____

_____

_____

Day 42 _____ (date)

I am

_____

_____

Today, I will

_____

_____

Today, I

_____

_____

My overall thoughts about my day:

_____

_____

_____

_____

_____

Day 43 _____ (date)

I am

_____

_____

Today, I will

_____

_____

Today, I

_____

_____

My overall thoughts about my day:

_____

_____

_____

_____

_____

Day 44 _____ (date)

I am

_____

_____

Today, I will

_____

_____

Today, I

_____

_____

My overall thoughts about my day:

_____

_____

_____

_____

_____

Day 45 _____ (date)

I am

_____

_____

Today, I will

_____

_____

Today, I

_____

_____

My overall thoughts about my day:

_____

_____

_____

_____

_____

Day 46 _____ (date)

I am

_____

_____

Today, I will

_____

_____

Today, I

_____

_____

My overall thoughts about my day:

_____

_____

_____

_____

_____

Day 47 _____ (date)

I am

_____

_____

Today, I will

_____

_____

Today, I

_____

_____

My overall thoughts about my day:

_____

_____

_____

_____

_____

Day 48 _____ (date)

I am

_____

_____

Today, I will

_____

_____

Today, I

_____

_____

My overall thoughts about my day:

_____

_____

_____

_____

_____

Day 49 _____ (date)

I am

_____

_____

Today, I will

_____

_____

Today, I

_____

_____

My overall thoughts about my day:

_____

_____

_____

_____

_____

Day 50 _____ (date)

I am

_____

_____

Today, I will

_____

_____

Today, I

_____

_____

My overall thoughts about my day:

_____

_____

_____

_____

_____

Day 51 _____ (date)

I am

_____

_____

Today, I will

_____

_____

Today, I

_____

_____

My overall thoughts about my day:

_____

_____

_____

_____

_____

Day 52 _____ (date)

I am

_____

_____

Today, I will

_____

_____

Today, I

_____

_____

My overall thoughts about my day:

_____

_____

_____

_____

_____

Day 53 _____ (date)

I am

_____

_____

Today, I will

_____

_____

Today, I

_____

_____

My overall thoughts about my day:

_____

_____

_____

_____

_____

Day 54 _____ (date)

I am

_____

_____

Today, I will

_____

_____

Today, I

_____

_____

My overall thoughts about my day:

_____

_____

_____

_____

_____

Day 55 _____ (date)

I am

_____

_____

Today, I will

_____

_____

Today, I

_____

_____

My overall thoughts about my day:

_____

_____

_____

_____

_____

Day 56 _____ (date)

I am

_____

_____

Today, I will

_____

_____

Today, I

_____

_____

My overall thoughts about my day:

_____

_____

_____

_____

_____

Day 57 _____ (date)

I am

_____
_____

Today, I will

_____
_____

Today, I

_____
_____

My overall thoughts about my day:

_____
_____
_____
_____
_____

Day 58 _____ (date)

I am

_____

_____

Today, I will

_____

_____

Today, I

_____

_____

My overall thoughts about my day:

_____

_____

_____

_____

_____

Day 59 _____ (date)

I am

_____

_____

Today, I will

_____

_____

Today, I

_____

_____

My overall thoughts about my day:

_____

_____

_____

_____

_____

Day 60 _____ (date)

I am

_____

_____

Today, I will

_____

_____

Today, I

_____

_____

My overall thoughts about my day:

_____

_____

_____

_____

_____

BE UNIQUE

Day 61 _____ (date)

I am

_____

_____

Today, I will

_____

_____

Today, I

_____

_____

My overall thoughts about my day:

_____

_____

_____

_____

_____

Day 62 _____ (date)

I am

_____

_____

Today, I will

_____

_____

Today, I

_____

_____

My overall thoughts about my day:

_____

_____

_____

_____

_____

BE UNIQUE

Day 63 _____ (date)

I am

_____

_____

Today, I will

_____

_____

Today, I

_____

_____

My overall thoughts about my day:

_____

_____

_____

_____

_____

Day 64 _____ (date)

I am

_____

_____

Today, I will

_____

_____

Today, I

_____

_____

My overall thoughts about my day:

_____

_____

_____

_____

_____

Day 65 _____ (date)

I am

_____

_____

Today, I will

_____

_____

Today, I

_____

_____

My overall thoughts about my day:

_____

_____

_____

_____

_____

BE UNIQUE

Day 66 _____ (date)

I am

_____

_____

Today, I will

_____

_____

Today, I

_____

_____

My overall thoughts about my day:

_____

_____

_____

_____

_____

Day 67 _____ (date)

I am

_____

_____

Today, I will

_____

_____

Today, I

_____

_____

My overall thoughts about my day:

_____

_____

_____

_____

_____

Day 68 _____ (date)

I am

_____

_____

Today, I will

_____

_____

Today, I

_____

_____

My overall thoughts about my day:

_____

_____

_____

_____

_____

Day 69 _____ (date)

I am

_____

_____

Today, I will

_____

_____

Today, I

_____

_____

My overall thoughts about my day:

_____

_____

_____

_____

_____

Day 70 _____ (date)

I am

_____

_____

Today, I will

_____

_____

Today, I

_____

_____

My overall thoughts about my day:

_____

_____

_____

_____

_____

Day 71 _____ (date)

I am

_____

_____

Today, I will

_____

_____

Today, I

_____

_____

My overall thoughts about my day:

_____

_____

_____

_____

_____

Day 72 _____ (date)

I am

_____

_____

Today, I will

_____

_____

Today, I

_____

_____

My overall thoughts about my day:

_____

_____

_____

_____

_____

Day 73 _____ (date)

I am

_____

_____

Today, I will

_____

_____

Today, I

_____

_____

My overall thoughts about my day:

_____

_____

_____

_____

_____

Day 74 _____ (date)

I am

_____

_____

Today, I will

_____

_____

Today, I

_____

_____

My overall thoughts about my day:

_____

_____

_____

_____

_____

Day 75 _____ (date)

I am

_____

_____

Today, I will

_____

_____

Today, I

_____

_____

My overall thoughts about my day:

_____

_____

_____

_____

_____

Day 76 _____ (date)

I am

_____

_____

Today, I will

_____

_____

Today, I

_____

_____

My overall thoughts about my day:

_____

_____

_____

_____

_____

BE UNIQUE

Day 77 _____ (date)

I am

_____

_____

Today, I will

_____

_____

Today, I

_____

_____

My overall thoughts about my day:

_____

_____

_____

_____

_____

Day 78 _____ (date)

I am

_____

_____

Today, I will

_____

_____

Today, I

_____

_____

My overall thoughts about my day:

_____

_____

_____

_____

_____

Day 79 _____ (date)

I am

_____

_____

Today, I will

_____

_____

Today, I

_____

_____

My overall thoughts about my day:

_____

_____

_____

_____

_____

Day 80 _____ (date)

I am

_____

_____

Today, I will

_____

_____

Today, I

_____

_____

My overall thoughts about my day:

_____

_____

_____

_____

_____

BE UNIQUE

Day 81 _____ (date)

I am

_____

_____

Today, I will

_____

_____

Today, I

_____

_____

My overall thoughts about my day:

_____

_____

_____

_____

_____

Day 82 _____ (date)

I am

_____

_____

Today, I will

_____

_____

Today, I

_____

_____

My overall thoughts about my day:

_____

_____

_____

_____

_____

BE UNIQUE

Day 83 _____ (date)

I am

_____

_____

Today, I will

_____

_____

Today, I

_____

_____

My overall thoughts about my day:

_____

_____

_____

_____

_____

BE UNIQUE

Day 84 _____ (date)

I am

_____

_____

Today, I will

_____

_____

Today, I

_____

_____

My overall thoughts about my day:

_____

_____

_____

_____

_____

Day 85_____ (date)

I am

_____

_____

Today, I will

_____

_____

Today, I

_____

_____

My overall thoughts about my day:

_____

_____

_____

_____

_____

Day 86 _____ (date)

I am

_____

_____

Today, I will

_____

_____

Today, I

_____

_____

My overall thoughts about my day:

_____

_____

_____

_____

_____

Day 87 _____ (date)

I am

_____

_____

Today, I will

_____

_____

Today, I

_____

_____

My overall thoughts about my day:

_____

_____

_____

_____

_____

Day 88 _____ (date)

I am

_____

_____

Today, I will

_____

_____

Today, I

_____

_____

My overall thoughts about my day:

_____

_____

_____

_____

_____

BE UNIQUE

Day 89 _____ (date)

I am

_____

_____

Today, I will

_____

_____

Today, I

_____

_____

My overall thoughts about my day:

_____

_____

_____

_____

_____

Day 90 _____ (date)

I am

_____

_____

Today, I will

_____

_____

Today, I

_____

_____

My overall thoughts about my day:

_____

_____

_____

_____

_____

Day 91 _____ (date)

I am

_____

_____

Today, I will

_____

_____

Today, I

_____

_____

My overall thoughts about my day:

_____

_____

_____

_____

_____

Day 92 _____ (date)

I am

_____

_____

Today, I will

_____

_____

Today, I

_____

_____

My overall thoughts about my day:

_____

_____

_____

_____

_____

Day 93 _____ (date)

I am

_____

_____

Today, I will

_____

_____

Today, I

_____

_____

My overall thoughts about my day:

_____

_____

_____

_____

_____

BE UNIQUE

Day 94 _____ (date)

I am

_____

_____

Today, I will

_____

_____

Today, I

_____

_____

My overall thoughts about my day:

_____

_____

_____

_____

_____

BE UNIQUE

Day 95 _____ (date)

I am

_____

_____

Today, I will

_____

_____

Today, I

_____

_____

My overall thoughts about my day:

_____

_____

_____

_____

_____

BE UNIQUE

Day 96 _____ (date)

I am

_____

_____

Today, I will

_____

_____

Today, I

_____

_____

My overall thoughts about my day:

_____

_____

_____

_____

_____

Day 97 _____ (date)

I am

_____

_____

Today, I will

_____

_____

Today, I

_____

_____

My overall thoughts about my day:

_____

_____

_____

_____

_____

Day 98 _____ (date)

I am

_____

_____

Today, I will

_____

_____

Today, I

_____

_____

My overall thoughts about my day:

_____

_____

_____

_____

_____

Day 99 _____ (date)

I am

_____

_____

Today, I will

_____

_____

Today, I

_____

_____

My overall thoughts about my day:

_____

_____

_____

_____

_____

Day 100 _____ (date)

I am

_____

_____

Today, I will

_____

_____

Today, I

_____

_____

My overall thoughts about my day:

_____

_____

_____

_____

_____

BE UNIQUE

Day 101 _____ (date)

I am

_____

_____

Today, I will

_____

_____

Today, I

_____

_____

My overall thoughts about my day:

_____

_____

_____

_____

_____

Day 102 _____ (date)

I am

_____

_____

Today, I will

_____

_____

Today, I

_____

_____

My overall thoughts about my day:

_____

_____

_____

_____

_____

Day 103 _____ (date)

I am

_____

_____

Today, I will

_____

_____

Today, I

_____

_____

My overall thoughts about my day:

_____

_____

_____

_____

_____

Day 104 _____ (date)

I am

_____

_____

Today, I will

_____

_____

Today, I

_____

_____

My overall thoughts about my day:

_____

_____

_____

_____

_____

Day 105 _____ (date)

I am

_____

_____

Today, I will

_____

_____

Today, I

_____

_____

My overall thoughts about my day:

_____

_____

_____

_____

_____

Day 106 _____ (date)

I am

_____

_____

Today, I will

_____

_____

Today, I

_____

_____

My overall thoughts about my day:

_____

_____

_____

_____

Day 107 _____ (date)

I am

_____

_____

Today, I will

_____

_____

Today, I

_____

_____

My overall thoughts about my day:

_____

_____

_____

_____

_____

Day 108 _____ (date)

I am

_____

_____

Today, I will

_____

_____

Today, I

_____

_____

My overall thoughts about my day:

_____

_____

_____

_____

_____

Day 109 _____ (date)

I am

_____

_____

Today, I will

_____

_____

Today, I

_____

_____

My overall thoughts about my day:

_____

_____

_____

_____

Day 110 _____ (date)

I am

_____

_____

Today, I will

_____

_____

Today, I

_____

_____

My overall thoughts about my day:

_____

_____

_____

_____

_____

Day 111 _____ (date)

I am

_____

_____

Today, I will

_____

_____

Today, I

_____

_____

My overall thoughts about my day:

_____

_____

_____

_____

_____

Day 112 _____ (date)

I am

_____

_____

Today, I will

_____

_____

Today, I

_____

_____

My overall thoughts about my day:

_____

_____

_____

_____

_____

BE UNIQUE

Day 113 _____ (date)

I am

_____

_____

Today, I will

_____

_____

Today, I

_____

_____

My overall thoughts about my day:

_____

_____

_____

_____

BE UNIQUE

Day 114 _____ (date)

I am

_____

_____

Today, I will

_____

_____

Today, I

_____

_____

My overall thoughts about my day:

_____

_____

_____

_____

_____

BE
UNIQUE

Day 115 _____ (date)

I am

_____

_____

Today, I will

_____

_____

Today, I

_____

_____

My overall thoughts about my day:

_____

_____

_____

_____

_____

Day 116 _____ (date)

I am

_____

_____

Today, I will

_____

_____

Today, I

_____

_____

My overall thoughts about my day:

_____

_____

_____

_____

_____

Be Unique

BE UNIQUE

Day 117 _____ (date)

I am

_____

_____

Today, I will

_____

_____

Today, I

_____

_____

My overall thoughts about my day:

_____

_____

_____

_____

_____

Day 118 _____ (date)

I am

_____

_____

Today, I will

_____

_____

Today, I

_____

_____

My overall thoughts about my day:

_____

_____

_____

_____

_____

Day 119 _____ (date)

I am

_____

_____

Today, I will

_____

_____

Today, I

_____

_____

My overall thoughts about my day:

_____

_____

_____

_____

_____

Day 120 _____ (date)

I am

_____

_____

Today, I will

_____

_____

Today, I

_____

_____

My overall thoughts about my day:

_____

_____

_____

_____

_____

Day 121 _____ (date)

I am

_____

_____

Today, I will

_____

_____

Today, I

_____

_____

My overall thoughts about my day:

_____

_____

_____

_____

Day 122 _____ (date)

I am

_____

_____

Today, I will

_____

_____

Today, I

_____

_____

My overall thoughts about my day:

_____

_____

_____

_____

_____

Day 123 _____ (date)

I am

_____

_____

Today, I will

_____

_____

Today, I

_____

_____

My overall thoughts about my day:

_____

_____

_____

_____

_____

Day 124 _____ (date)

I am

_____

_____

Today, I will

_____

_____

Today, I

_____

_____

My overall thoughts about my day:

_____

_____

_____

_____

_____

Day 125 _____ (date)

I am

_____

_____

Today, I will

_____

_____

Today, I

_____

_____

My overall thoughts about my day:

_____

_____

_____

_____

_____

Day 126 _____ (date)

I am

_____

_____

Today, I will

_____

_____

Today, I

_____

_____

My overall thoughts about my day:

_____

_____

_____

_____

_____

Day 127 _____ (date)

I am

_____

_____

Today, I will

_____

_____

Today, I

_____

_____

My overall thoughts about my day:

_____

_____

_____

_____

_____

Day 128 _____ (date)

I am

_____

_____

Today, I will

_____

_____

Today, I

_____

_____

My overall thoughts about my day:

_____

_____

_____

_____

_____

Day 129 _____ (date)

I am

_____

_____

Today, I will

_____

_____

Today, I

_____

_____

My overall thoughts about my day:

_____

_____

_____

_____

_____

Day 130 _____ (date)

I am

_____

_____

Today, I will

_____

_____

Today, I

_____

_____

My overall thoughts about my day:

_____

_____

_____

_____

_____

BE UNIQUE

Day 131 _____ (date)

I am

_____

_____

Today, I will

_____

_____

Today, I

_____

_____

My overall thoughts about my day:

_____

_____

_____

_____

_____

Day 132 _____ (date)

I am

_____

_____

Today, I will

_____

_____

Today, I

_____

_____

My overall thoughts about my day:

_____

_____

_____

_____

_____

Day 133 _____ (date)

I am

_____

_____

Today, I will

_____

_____

Today, I

_____

_____

My overall thoughts about my day:

_____

_____

_____

_____

_____

Day 134 _____ (date)

I am

_____

_____

Today, I will

_____

_____

Today, I

_____

_____

My overall thoughts about my day:

_____

_____

_____

_____

_____

Day 135 _____ (date)

I am

_____

_____

Today, I will

_____

_____

Today, I

_____

_____

My overall thoughts about my day:

_____

_____

_____

_____

_____

Day 136 _____ (date)

I am

_____

_____

Today, I will

_____

_____

Today, I

_____

_____

My overall thoughts about my day:

_____

_____

_____

_____

_____

BE UNIQUE

Day 137 _____ (date)

I am

_____

_____

Today, I will

_____

_____

Today, I

_____

_____

My overall thoughts about my day:

_____

_____

_____

_____

_____

Day 138 _____ (date)

I am

_____

_____

Today, I will

_____

_____

Today, I

_____

_____

My overall thoughts about my day:

_____

_____

_____

_____

_____

Day 139 _____ (date)

I am

_____

_____

Today, I will

_____

_____

Today, I

_____

_____

My overall thoughts about my day:

_____

_____

_____

_____

_____

Day 140 _____ (date)

I am

_____

_____

Today, I will

_____

_____

Today, I

_____

_____

My overall thoughts about my day:

_____

_____

_____

_____

_____

Day 141 _____ (date)

I am

_____

_____

Today, I will

_____

_____

Today, I

_____

_____

My overall thoughts about my day:

_____

_____

_____

_____

_____

Day 142 _____ (date)

I am

_____

_____

Today, I will

_____

_____

Today, I

_____

_____

My overall thoughts about my day:

_____

_____

_____

_____

_____

Day 143 _____ (date)

I am

_____

_____

Today, I will

_____

_____

Today, I

_____

_____

My overall thoughts about my day:

_____

_____

_____

_____

_____

Day 144 _____ (date)

I am

_____

_____

Today, I will

_____

_____

Today, I

_____

_____

My overall thoughts about my day:

_____

_____

_____

_____

_____

BE
UNIQUE

Day 145 _____ (date)

I am

_____

_____

Today, I will

_____

_____

Today, I

_____

_____

My overall thoughts about my day:

_____

_____

_____

_____

_____

Day 146 _____ (date)

I am

_____

_____

Today, I will

_____

_____

Today, I

_____

_____

My overall thoughts about my day:

_____

_____

_____

_____

_____

BE
UNIQUE

Day 147 _____ (date)

I am

_____

_____

Today, I will

_____

_____

Today, I

_____

_____

My overall thoughts about my day:

_____

_____

_____

_____

_____

Day 148 _____ (date)

I am

_____

_____

Today, I will

_____

_____

Today, I

_____

_____

My overall thoughts about my day:

_____

_____

_____

_____

Day 149 _____ (date)

I am

_____

_____

Today, I will

_____

_____

Today, I

_____

_____

My overall thoughts about my day:

_____

_____

_____

_____

_____

BE UNIQUE

Day 150 _____ (date)

I am

_____

_____

Today, I will

_____

_____

Today, I

_____

_____

My overall thoughts about my day:

_____

_____

_____

_____

_____

Day 151 _____ (date)

I am

_____

_____

Today, I will

_____

_____

Today, I

_____

_____

My overall thoughts about my day:

_____

_____

_____

_____

_____

Day 152 _____ (date)

I am

_____

_____

Today, I will

_____

_____

Today, I

_____

_____

My overall thoughts about my day:

_____

_____

_____

_____

_____

BE UNIQUE

Day 153 _____ (date)

I am

_____

_____

Today, I will

_____

_____

Today, I

_____

_____

My overall thoughts about my day:

_____

_____

_____

_____

_____

Day 154 _____ (date)

I am

_____

_____

Today, I will

_____

_____

Today, I

_____

_____

My overall thoughts about my day:

_____

_____

_____

_____

_____

Day 155 _____ (date)

I am

_____

_____

Today, I will

_____

_____

Today, I

_____

_____

My overall thoughts about my day:

_____

_____

_____

_____

_____

Day 156 _____ (date)

I am

_____

_____

Today, I will

_____

_____

Today, I

_____

_____

My overall thoughts about my day:

_____

_____

_____

_____

_____

Day 157 _____ (date)

I am

_____

_____

Today, I will

_____

_____

Today, I

_____

_____

My overall thoughts about my day:

_____

_____

_____

_____

_____

Day 158 _____ (date)

I am

_____

_____

Today, I will

_____

_____

Today, I

_____

_____

My overall thoughts about my day:

_____

_____

_____

_____

_____

Day 159 _____ (date)

I am

_____

_____

Today, I will

_____

_____

Today, I

_____

_____

My overall thoughts about my day:

_____

_____

_____

_____

_____

Day 160 _____ (date)

I am

_____

_____

Today, I will

_____

_____

Today, I

_____

_____

My overall thoughts about my day:

_____

_____

_____

_____

_____

Day 161 _____ (date)

I am

_____

_____

Today, I will

_____

_____

Today, I

_____

_____

My overall thoughts about my day:

_____

_____

_____

_____

_____

Day 162 _____ (date)

I am

_____
_____

Today, I will

_____
_____

Today, I

_____
_____

My overall thoughts about my day:

_____
_____
_____
_____
_____

Day 163 _____ (date)

I am

_____

_____

Today, I will

_____

_____

Today, I

_____

_____

My overall thoughts about my day:

_____

_____

_____

_____

_____

Day 164 _____ (date)

I am

_____

_____

Today, I will

_____

_____

Today, I

_____

_____

My overall thoughts about my day:

_____

_____

_____

_____

_____

Day 165 _____ (date)

I am

_____

_____

Today, I will

_____

_____

Today, I

_____

_____

My overall thoughts about my day:

_____

_____

_____

_____

_____

Day 166 _____ (date)

I am

_____

_____

Today, I will

_____

_____

Today, I

_____

_____

My overall thoughts about my day:

_____

_____

_____

_____

_____

BE UNIQUE

Day 167 _____ (date)

I am

_____

_____

Today, I will

_____

_____

Today, I

_____

_____

My overall thoughts about my day:

_____

_____

_____

_____

_____

Day 168 _____ (date)

I am

_____

_____

Today, I will

_____

_____

Today, I

_____

_____

My overall thoughts about my day:

_____

_____

_____

_____

_____

Day 169 _____ (date)

I am

_____

_____

Today, I will

_____

_____

Today, I

_____

_____

My overall thoughts about my day:

_____

_____

_____

_____

_____

Day 170 _____ (date)

I am

_____

_____

Today, I will

_____

_____

Today, I

_____

_____

My overall thoughts about my day:

_____

_____

_____

_____

_____

Day 171 _____ (date)

I am

_____

_____

Today, I will

_____

_____

Today, I

_____

_____

My overall thoughts about my day:

_____

_____

_____

_____

_____

Day 172 _____ (date)

I am

_____

_____

Today, I will

_____

_____

Today, I

_____

_____

My overall thoughts about my day:

_____

_____

_____

_____

_____

BE UNIQUE

Day 173 _____ (date)

I am

_____

_____

Today, I will

_____

_____

Today, I

_____

_____

My overall thoughts about my day:

_____

_____

_____

_____

_____

BE UNIQUE

Day 174 _____ (date)

I am

_____

_____

Today, I will

_____

_____

Today, I

_____

_____

My overall thoughts about my day:

_____

_____

_____

_____

_____

Day 175 _____ (date)

I am

_____

_____

Today, I will

_____

_____

Today, I

_____

_____

My overall thoughts about my day:

_____

_____

_____

_____

_____

Day 176 _____ (date)

I am

_____

_____

Today, I will

_____

_____

Today, I

_____

_____

My overall thoughts about my day:

_____

_____

_____

_____

_____

Day 177 _____ (date)

I am

_____

_____

Today, I will

_____

_____

Today, I

_____

_____

My overall thoughts about my day:

_____

_____

_____

_____

_____

BE UNIQUE

Day 178 _____ (date)

I am

_____

_____

Today, I will

_____

_____

Today, I

_____

_____

My overall thoughts about my day:

_____

_____

_____

_____

_____

BE UNIQUE

Day 179 _____ (date)

I am

_____

_____

Today, I will

_____

_____

Today, I

_____

_____

My overall thoughts about my day:

_____

_____

_____

_____

_____

Day 180 _____ (date)

I am

_____

_____

Today, I will

_____

_____

Today, I

_____

_____

My overall thoughts about my day:

_____

_____

_____

_____

_____

Day 181 _____ (date)

I am

_____

_____

Today, I will

_____

_____

Today, I

_____

_____

My overall thoughts about my day:

_____

_____

_____

_____

_____

BE UNIQUE

Day 182 _____ (date)

I am

_____

_____

Today, I will

_____

_____

Today, I

_____

_____

My overall thoughts about my day:

_____

_____

_____

_____

_____

Day 183 _____ (date)

I am

_____

_____

Today, I will

_____

_____

Today, I

_____

_____

My overall thoughts about my day:

_____

_____

_____

_____

_____

Day 184 _____ (date)

I am

_____

_____

Today, I will

_____

_____

Today, I

_____

_____

My overall thoughts about my day:

_____

_____

_____

_____

_____

BE UNIQUE

Day 185 _____ (date)

I am

_____

_____

Today, I will

_____

_____

Today, I

_____

_____

My overall thoughts about my day:

_____

_____

_____

_____

_____

Day 186 _____ (date)

I am

_____

_____

Today, I will

_____

_____

Today, I

_____

_____

My overall thoughts about my day:

_____

_____

_____

_____

_____

Day 187 _____ (date)

I am

_____

_____

Today, I will

_____

_____

Today, I

_____

_____

My overall thoughts about my day:

_____

_____

_____

_____

BE UNIQUE

Day 188 _____ (date)

I am

_____

_____

Today, I will

_____

_____

Today, I

_____

_____

My overall thoughts about my day:

_____

_____

_____

_____

_____

Day 189 _____ (date)

I am

_____

_____

Today, I will

_____

_____

Today, I

_____

_____

My overall thoughts about my day:

_____

_____

_____

_____

Day 190 _____ (date)

I am

_____

_____

Today, I will

_____

_____

Today, I

_____

_____

My overall thoughts about my day:

_____

_____

_____

_____

_____

BE UNIQUE

Day 191 _____ (date)

I am

_____

_____

Today, I will

_____

_____

Today, I

_____

_____

My overall thoughts about my day:

_____

_____

_____

_____

_____

Day 192 _____ (date)

I am

_____

_____

Today, I will

_____

_____

Today, I

_____

_____

My overall thoughts about my day:

_____

_____

_____

_____

Day 193 _____ (date)

I am

_____

_____

Today, I will

_____

_____

Today, I

_____

_____

My overall thoughts about my day:

_____

_____

_____

_____

_____

Day 194 _____ (date)

I am

_____

_____

Today, I will

_____

_____

Today, I

_____

_____

My overall thoughts about my day:

_____

_____

_____

_____

_____

Day 195 _____ (date)

I am

_____

_____

Today, I will

_____

_____

Today, I

_____

_____

My overall thoughts about my day:

_____

_____

_____

_____

_____

Day 196 _____ (date)

I am

_____

_____

Today, I will

_____

_____

Today, I

_____

_____

My overall thoughts about my day:

_____

_____

_____

_____

_____

Day 197 _____ (date)

I am

_____

_____

Today, I will

_____

_____

Today, I

_____

_____

My overall thoughts about my day:

_____

_____

_____

_____

_____

Day 198 _____ (date)

I am

_____

_____

Today, I will

_____

_____

Today, I

_____

_____

My overall thoughts about my day:

_____

_____

_____

_____

_____

Day 199 _____ (date)

I am

_____

_____

Today, I will

_____

_____

Today, I

_____

_____

My overall thoughts about my day:

_____

_____

_____

_____

_____

Day 200 _____ (date)

I am

_____

_____

Today, I will

_____

_____

Today, I

_____

_____

My overall thoughts about my day:

_____

_____

_____

_____

_____

Day 201 _____ (date)

I am

_____

_____

Today, I will

_____

_____

Today, I

_____

_____

My overall thoughts about my day:

_____

_____

_____

_____

_____

Day 202 _____ (date)

I am

_____

_____

Today, I will

_____

_____

Today, I

_____

_____

My overall thoughts about my day:

_____

_____

_____

_____

_____

Day 203 _____ (date)

I am

_____

_____

Today, I will

_____

_____

Today, I

_____

_____

My overall thoughts about my day:

_____

_____

_____

_____

_____

Day 204 _____ (date)

I am

_____

_____

Today, I will

_____

_____

Today, I

_____

_____

My overall thoughts about my day:

_____

_____

_____

_____

_____

Day 205 _____ (date)

I am

_____

_____

Today, I will

_____

_____

Today, I

_____

_____

My overall thoughts about my day:

_____

_____

_____

_____

_____

BE UNIQUE

Day 206 _____ (date)

I am

_____

_____

Today, I will

_____

_____

Today, I

_____

_____

My overall thoughts about my day:

_____

_____

_____

_____

Day 207_____ (date)

I am

_____

_____

Today, I will

_____

_____

Today, I

_____

_____

My overall thoughts about my day:

_____

_____

_____

_____

_____

Day 208 _____ (date)

I am

_____

_____

Today, I will

_____

_____

Today, I

_____

_____

My overall thoughts about my day:

_____

_____

_____

_____

_____

Day 209 _____ (date)

I am

_____

_____

Today, I will

_____

_____

Today, I

_____

_____

My overall thoughts about my day:

_____

_____

_____

_____

_____

Day 210 _____ (date)

I am

_____
_____

Today, I will

_____
_____

Today, I

_____
_____

My overall thoughts about my day:

_____
_____
_____
_____
_____

BE
UNIQUE

Day 211 _____ (date)

I am

_____

_____

Today, I will

_____

_____

Today, I

_____

_____

My overall thoughts about my day:

_____

_____

_____

_____

_____

Day 212 _____ (date)

I am

_____

_____

Today, I will

_____

_____

Today, I

_____

_____

My overall thoughts about my day:

_____

_____

_____

_____

_____

Day 213 _____ (date)

I am

_____

_____

Today, I will

_____

_____

Today, I

_____

_____

My overall thoughts about my day:

_____

_____

_____

_____

_____

Day 214 _____ (date)

I am

_____

_____

Today, I will

_____

_____

Today, I

_____

_____

My overall thoughts about my day:

_____

_____

_____

_____

_____

BE UNIQUE

Day 215 _____ (date)

I am

_____

_____

Today, I will

_____

_____

Today, I

_____

_____

My overall thoughts about my day:

_____

_____

_____

_____

_____

BE UNIQUE

Day 216 _____ (date)

I am

_____

_____

Today, I will

_____

_____

Today, I

_____

_____

My overall thoughts about my day:

_____

_____

_____

_____

_____

Day 217 _____ (date)

I am

_____

_____

Today, I will

_____

_____

Today, I

_____

_____

My overall thoughts about my day:

_____

_____

_____

_____

_____

Day 218 _____ (date)

I am

_____

_____

Today, I will

_____

_____

Today, I

_____

_____

My overall thoughts about my day:

_____

_____

_____

_____

_____

Day 219 _____ (date)

I am

_____

_____

Today, I will

_____

_____

Today, I

_____

_____

My overall thoughts about my day:

_____

_____

_____

_____

_____

Day 220 _____ (date)

I am

_____

_____

Today, I will

_____

_____

Today, I

_____

_____

My overall thoughts about my day:

_____

_____

_____

_____

_____

Day 221 _____ (date)

I am

_____

_____

Today, I will

_____

_____

Today, I

_____

_____

My overall thoughts about my day:

_____

_____

_____

_____

_____

Day 222 _____ (date)

I am

_____

_____

Today, I will

_____

_____

Today, I

_____

_____

My overall thoughts about my day:

_____

_____

_____

_____

_____

BE UNIQUE

Day 223 _____ (date)

I am

_____

_____

Today, I will

_____

_____

Today, I

_____

_____

My overall thoughts about my day:

_____

_____

_____

_____

_____

Day 224 _____ (date)

I am

_____

_____

Today, I will

_____

_____

Today, I

_____

_____

My overall thoughts about my day:

_____

_____

_____

_____

Be Unique

Day 225 _____ (date)

I am

_____

_____

Today, I will

_____

_____

Today, I

_____

_____

My overall thoughts about my day:

_____

_____

_____

_____

_____

Day 226 _____ (date)

I am

_____

_____

Today, I will

_____

_____

Today, I

_____

_____

My overall thoughts about my day:

_____

_____

_____

_____

_____

BE UNIQUE

Day 227 _____ (date)

I am

_____

_____

Today, I will

_____

_____

Today, I

_____

_____

My overall thoughts about my day:

_____

_____

_____

_____

Day 228 _____ (date)

I am

_____

_____

Today, I will

_____

_____

Today, I

_____

_____

My overall thoughts about my day:

_____

_____

_____

_____

_____

Day 229 _____ (date)

I am

_____

_____

Today, I will

_____

_____

Today, I

_____

_____

My overall thoughts about my day:

_____

_____

_____

_____

_____

Day 230 _____ (date)

I am

_____

_____

Today, I will

_____

_____

Today, I

_____

_____

My overall thoughts about my day:

_____

_____

_____

_____

_____

BE UNIQUE

Day 231 _____ (date)

I am

_____

_____

Today, I will

_____

_____

Today, I

_____

_____

My overall thoughts about my day:

_____

_____

_____

_____

_____

Day 232 _____ (date)

I am

_____
_____

Today, I will

_____
_____

Today, I

_____
_____

My overall thoughts about my day:

_____
_____
_____
_____
_____

BE UNIQUE

Day 233 _____ (date)

I am

_____

_____

Today, I will

_____

_____

Today, I

_____

_____

My overall thoughts about my day:

_____

_____

_____

_____

_____

Day 234 _____ (date)

I am

_____

_____

Today, I will

_____

_____

Today, I

_____

_____

My overall thoughts about my day:

_____

_____

_____

_____

_____

Day 235 _____ (date)

I am

_____

_____

Today, I will

_____

_____

Today, I

_____

_____

My overall thoughts about my day:

_____

_____

_____

_____

_____

Day 236 _____ (date)

I am

_____

_____

Today, I will

_____

_____

Today, I

_____

_____

My overall thoughts about my day:

_____

_____

_____

_____

Day 237 _____ (date)

I am

_____

_____

Today, I will

_____

_____

Today, I

_____

_____

My overall thoughts about my day:

_____

_____

_____

_____

_____

Day 238 _____ (date)

I am

_____
_____

Today, I will

_____
_____

Today, I

_____
_____

My overall thoughts about my day:

_____
_____
_____
_____
_____

Day 239 _____ (date)

I am

_____

_____

Today, I will

_____

_____

Today, I

_____

_____

My overall thoughts about my day:

_____

_____

_____

_____

_____

Day 240 _____ (date)

I am

_____

_____

Today, I will

_____

_____

Today, I

_____

_____

My overall thoughts about my day:

_____

_____

_____

_____

_____

BE UNIQUE

Day 241 _____ (date)

I am

_____

_____

Today, I will

_____

_____

Today, I

_____

_____

My overall thoughts about my day:

_____

_____

_____

_____

Day 242 _____ (date)

I am

_____

_____

Today, I will

_____

_____

Today, I

_____

_____

My overall thoughts about my day:

_____

_____

_____

_____

_____

Day 243 _____ (date)

I am

_____

_____

Today, I will

_____

_____

Today, I

_____

_____

My overall thoughts about my day:

_____

_____

_____

_____

_____

Day 244 _____ (date)

I am

_____

_____

Today, I will

_____

_____

Today, I

_____

_____

My overall thoughts about my day:

_____

_____

_____

_____

_____

Day 245 _____ (date)

I am

_____

_____

Today, I will

_____

_____

Today, I

_____

_____

My overall thoughts about my day:

_____

_____

_____

_____

_____

Day 246 _____ (date)

I am

_____

_____

Today, I will

_____

_____

Today, I

_____

_____

My overall thoughts about my day:

_____

_____

_____

_____

_____

BE UNIQUE

Day 247 _____ (date)

I am

_____

_____

Today, I will

_____

_____

Today, I

_____

_____

My overall thoughts about my day:

_____

_____

_____

_____

_____

Day 248_____ (date)

I am

_____

_____

Today, I will

_____

_____

Today, I

_____

_____

My overall thoughts about my day:

_____

_____

_____

_____

_____

Day 249 _____ (date)

I am

_____

_____

Today, I will

_____

_____

Today, I

_____

_____

My overall thoughts about my day:

_____

_____

_____

_____

_____

Day 250 _____ (date)

I am

_____

_____

Today, I will

_____

_____

Today, I

_____

_____

My overall thoughts about my day:

_____

_____

_____

_____

_____

BE UNIQUE

Day 251 _____ (date)

I am

_____

_____

Today, I will

_____

_____

Today, I

_____

_____

My overall thoughts about my day:

_____

_____

_____

_____

_____

Day 252 _____ (date)

I am

_____

_____

Today, I will

_____

_____

Today, I

_____

_____

My overall thoughts about my day:

_____

_____

_____

_____

_____

BE UNIQUE

Day 253 _____ (date)

I am

_____

_____

Today, I will

_____

_____

Today, I

_____

_____

My overall thoughts about my day:

_____

_____

_____

_____

_____

Day 254 _____ (date)

I am

_____

_____

Today, I will

_____

_____

Today, I

_____

_____

My overall thoughts about my day:

_____

_____

_____

_____

_____

Day 255 _____ (date)

I am

_____

_____

Today, I will

_____

_____

Today, I

_____

_____

My overall thoughts about my day:

_____

_____

_____

_____

_____

Day 256 _____ (date)

I am

_____

_____

Today, I will

_____

_____

Today, I

_____

_____

My overall thoughts about my day:

_____

_____

_____

_____

_____

BE UNIQUE

Day 257 _____ (date)

I am

_____

_____

Today, I will

_____

_____

Today, I

_____

_____

My overall thoughts about my day:

_____

_____

_____

_____

_____

Day 258 _____ (date)

I am

_____

_____

Today, I will

_____

_____

Today, I

_____

_____

My overall thoughts about my day:

_____

_____

_____

_____

_____

Day 259 _____ (date)

I am

_____

_____

Today, I will

_____

_____

Today, I

_____

_____

My overall thoughts about my day:

_____

_____

_____

_____

Day 260 _____ (date)

I am

_____

_____

Today, I will

_____

_____

Today, I

_____

_____

My overall thoughts about my day:

_____

_____

_____

_____

_____

Day 261 _____ (date)

I am

_____

_____

Today, I will

_____

_____

Today, I

_____

_____

My overall thoughts about my day:

_____

_____

_____

_____

_____

Day 262 _____ (date)

I am

_____

_____

Today, I will

_____

_____

Today, I

_____

_____

My overall thoughts about my day:

_____

_____

_____

_____

Day 263_____ (date)

I am

_____

_____

Today, I will

_____

_____

Today, I

_____

_____

My overall thoughts about my day:

_____

_____

_____

_____

_____

Day 264 _____ (date)

I am

_____

_____

Today, I will

_____

_____

Today, I

_____

_____

My overall thoughts about my day:

_____

_____

_____

_____

_____

Day 265 _____ (date)

I am

_____

_____

Today, I will

_____

_____

Today, I

_____

_____

My overall thoughts about my day:

_____

_____

_____

_____

_____

Day 266 _____ (date)

I am

_____

_____

Today, I will

_____

_____

Today, I

_____

_____

My overall thoughts about my day:

_____

_____

_____

_____

_____

Be Unique

Day 267 _____ (date)

I am

_____

_____

Today, I will

_____

_____

Today, I

_____

_____

My overall thoughts about my day:

_____

_____

_____

_____

_____

Day 268 _____ (date)

I am

_____

_____

Today, I will

_____

_____

Today, I

_____

_____

My overall thoughts about my day:

_____

_____

_____

_____

_____

Day 269 _____ (date)

I am

_____

_____

Today, I will

_____

_____

Today, I

_____

_____

My overall thoughts about my day:

_____

_____

_____

_____

_____

Day 270 _____ (date)

I am

_____

_____

Today, I will

_____

_____

Today, I

_____

_____

My overall thoughts about my day:

_____

_____

_____

_____

_____

Day 271 _____ (date)

I am

_____

_____

Today, I will

_____

_____

Today, I

_____

_____

My overall thoughts about my day:

_____

_____

_____

_____

_____

Day 272 _____ (date)

I am

_____

_____

Today, I will

_____

_____

Today, I

_____

_____

My overall thoughts about my day:

_____

_____

_____

_____

_____

Day 273 _____ (date)

I am

_____

_____

Today, I will

_____

_____

Today, I

_____

_____

My overall thoughts about my day:

_____

_____

_____

_____

_____

Day 274 _____ (date)

I am

_____

_____

Today, I will

_____

_____

Today, I

_____

_____

My overall thoughts about my day:

_____

_____

_____

_____

_____

BE UNIQUE

Day 275 _____ (date)

I am

_____

_____

Today, I will

_____

_____

Today, I

_____

_____

My overall thoughts about my day:

_____

_____

_____

_____

_____

Day 276 _____ (date)

I am

_____

_____

Today, I will

_____

_____

Today, I

_____

_____

My overall thoughts about my day:

_____

_____

_____

_____

_____

BE UNIQUE

Day 277 _____ (date)

I am

_____

_____

Today, I will

_____

_____

Today, I

_____

_____

My overall thoughts about my day:

_____

_____

_____

_____

_____

Day 278 _____ (date)

I am

_____

_____

Today, I will

_____

_____

Today, I

_____

_____

My overall thoughts about my day:

_____

_____

_____

_____

_____

Day 279 _____ (date)

I am

_____

_____

Today, I will

_____

_____

Today, I

_____

_____

My overall thoughts about my day:

_____

_____

_____

_____

_____

Day 3280_____ (date)

I am

_____

_____

Today, I will

_____

_____

Today, I

_____

_____

My overall thoughts about my day:

_____

_____

_____

_____

_____

Day 281 _____ (date)

I am

_____

_____

Today, I will

_____

_____

Today, I

_____

_____

My overall thoughts about my day:

_____

_____

_____

_____

_____

Day 282 _____ (date)

I am

_____

_____

Today, I will

_____

_____

Today, I

_____

_____

My overall thoughts about my day:

_____

_____

_____

_____

_____

Day 283 _____ (date)

I am

_____

_____

Today, I will

_____

_____

Today, I

_____

_____

My overall thoughts about my day:

_____

_____

_____

_____

_____

Day 284 _____ (date)

I am

_____

_____

Today, I will

_____

_____

Today, I

_____

_____

My overall thoughts about my day:

_____

_____

_____

_____

_____

Day 285 _____ (date)

I am

_____

_____

Today, I will

_____

_____

Today, I

_____

_____

My overall thoughts about my day:

_____

_____

_____

_____

_____

Day 286 _____ (date)

I am

_____

_____

Today, I will

_____

_____

Today, I

_____

_____

My overall thoughts about my day:

_____

_____

_____

_____

_____

BE UNIQUE

Day 287_____ (date)

I am

_____

_____

Today, I will

_____

_____

Today, I

_____

_____

My overall thoughts about my day:

_____

_____

_____

_____

_____

Day 288 _____ (date)

I am

_____

_____

Today, I will

_____

_____

Today, I

_____

_____

My overall thoughts about my day:

_____

_____

_____

_____

_____

Day 289 _____ (date)

I am

_____

_____

Today, I will

_____

_____

Today, I

_____

_____

My overall thoughts about my day:

_____

_____

_____

_____

_____

Day 290 _____ (date)

I am

_____

_____

Today, I will

_____

_____

Today, I

_____

_____

My overall thoughts about my day:

_____

_____

_____

_____

Day 291 _____ (date)

I am

_____

_____

Today, I will

_____

_____

Today, I

_____

_____

My overall thoughts about my day:

_____

_____

_____

_____

_____

Day 292 _____ (date)

I am

_____

_____

Today, I will

_____

_____

Today, I

_____

_____

My overall thoughts about my day:

_____

_____

_____

_____

_____

Day 293 _____ (date)

I am

_____

_____

Today, I will

_____

_____

Today, I

_____

_____

My overall thoughts about my day:

_____

_____

_____

_____

_____

Day 294 _____ (date)

I am

_____

_____

Today, I will

_____

_____

Today, I

_____

_____

My overall thoughts about my day:

_____

_____

_____

_____

_____

Day 295_____ (date)

I am

_____

_____

Today, I will

_____

_____

Today, I

_____

_____

My overall thoughts about my day:

_____

_____

_____

_____

_____

Day 296 _____ (date)

I am

_____

_____

Today, I will

_____

_____

Today, I

_____

_____

My overall thoughts about my day:

_____

_____

_____

_____

_____

Day 297 _____ (date)

I am

_____

_____

Today, I will

_____

_____

Today, I

_____

_____

My overall thoughts about my day:

_____

_____

_____

_____

_____

Day 298 _____ (date)

I am

_____

_____

Today, I will

_____

_____

Today, I

_____

_____

My overall thoughts about my day:

_____

_____

_____

_____

_____

Day 299 _____ (date)

I am

_____

_____

Today, I will

_____

_____

Today, I

_____

_____

My overall thoughts about my day:

_____

_____

_____

_____

_____

Day 300 _____ (date)

I am

_____

_____

Today, I will

_____

_____

Today, I

_____

_____

My overall thoughts about my day:

_____

_____

_____

_____

_____

Day 301 _____ (date)

I am

_____

_____

Today, I will

_____

_____

Today, I

_____

_____

My overall thoughts about my day:

_____

_____

_____

_____

_____

Day 302 _____ (date)

I am

_____

_____

Today, I will

_____

_____

Today, I

_____

_____

My overall thoughts about my day:

_____

_____

_____

_____

_____

Day 303 _____ (date)

I am

_____

_____

Today, I will

_____

_____

Today, I

_____

_____

My overall thoughts about my day:

_____

_____

_____

_____

_____

Day 304 _____ (date)

I am

_____

_____

Today, I will

_____

_____

Today, I

_____

_____

My overall thoughts about my day:

_____

_____

_____

_____

_____

Day 305 _____ (date)

I am

_____

_____

Today, I will

_____

_____

Today, I

_____

_____

My overall thoughts about my day:

_____

_____

_____

_____

_____

Day 306 _____ (date)

I am

_____

_____

Today, I will

_____

_____

Today, I

_____

_____

My overall thoughts about my day:

_____

_____

_____

_____

_____

Day 307 _____ (date)

I am

_____

_____

Today, I will

_____

_____

Today, I

_____

_____

My overall thoughts about my day:

_____

_____

_____

_____

_____

Day 308 _____ (date)

I am

_____

_____

Today, I will

_____

_____

Today, I

_____

_____

My overall thoughts about my day:

_____

_____

_____

_____

_____

BE
UNIQUE

Day 309 _____ (date)

I am

_____

_____

Today, I will

_____

_____

Today, I

_____

_____

My overall thoughts about my day:

_____

_____

_____

_____

_____

Day 310 _____ (date)

I am

_____

_____

Today, I will

_____

_____

Today, I

_____

_____

My overall thoughts about my day:

_____

_____

_____

_____

_____

Be Unique

Day 311 _____ (date)

I am

_____

_____

Today, I will

_____

_____

Today, I

_____

_____

My overall thoughts about my day:

_____

_____

_____

_____

_____

Day 312 _____ (date)

I am

_____

_____

Today, I will

_____

_____

Today, I

_____

_____

My overall thoughts about my day:

_____

_____

_____

_____

_____

Day 313 _____ (date)

I am

_____

_____

Today, I will

_____

_____

Today, I

_____

_____

My overall thoughts about my day:

_____

_____

_____

_____

Day 314 _____ (date)

I am

_____

_____

Today, I will

_____

_____

Today, I

_____

_____

My overall thoughts about my day:

_____

_____

_____

_____

_____

Day 315 _____ (date)

I am

_____

_____

Today, I will

_____

_____

Today, I

_____

_____

My overall thoughts about my day:

_____

_____

_____

_____

_____

Day 316 _____ (date)

I am

_____

_____

Today, I will

_____

_____

Today, I

_____

_____

My overall thoughts about my day:

_____

_____

_____

_____

BE UNIQUE

Day 317 _____ (date)

I am

_____

_____

Today, I will

_____

_____

Today, I

_____

_____

My overall thoughts about my day:

_____

_____

_____

_____

_____

Day 318 _____ (date)

I am

_____

_____

Today, I will

_____

_____

Today, I

_____

_____

My overall thoughts about my day:

_____

_____

_____

_____

Day 319 _____ (date)

I am

_____

_____

Today, I will

_____

_____

Today, I

_____

_____

My overall thoughts about my day:

_____

_____

_____

_____

_____

Day 320 _____ (date)

I am

_____

_____

Today, I will

_____

_____

Today, I

_____

_____

My overall thoughts about my day:

_____

_____

_____

_____

_____

Day 321 _____ (date)

I am

_____

_____

Today, I will

_____

_____

Today, I

_____

_____

My overall thoughts about my day:

_____

_____

_____

_____

_____

Day 322 _____ (date)

I am

_____

_____

Today, I will

_____

_____

Today, I

_____

_____

My overall thoughts about my day:

_____

_____

_____

_____

BE UNIQUE

Day 323 _____ (date)

I am

_____

_____

Today, I will

_____

_____

Today, I

_____

_____

My overall thoughts about my day:

_____

_____

_____

_____

_____

Day 324 _____ (date)

I am

_____

_____

Today, I will

_____

_____

Today, I

_____

_____

My overall thoughts about my day:

_____

_____

_____

_____

_____

Day 325 _____ (date)

I am

_____

_____

Today, I will

_____

_____

Today, I

_____

_____

My overall thoughts about my day:

_____

_____

_____

_____

_____

Day 326 _____ (date)

I am

_____

_____

Today, I will

_____

_____

Today, I

_____

_____

My overall thoughts about my day:

_____

_____

_____

_____

_____

Day 327 _____ (date)

I am

_____

_____

Today, I will

_____

_____

Today, I

_____

_____

My overall thoughts about my day:

_____

_____

_____

_____

_____

Day 328 _____ (date)

I am

_____

_____

Today, I will

_____

_____

Today, I

_____

_____

My overall thoughts about my day:

_____

_____

_____

_____

_____

BE UNIQUE

Day 329 _____ (date)

I am

_____

_____

Today, I will

_____

_____

Today, I

_____

_____

My overall thoughts about my day:

_____

_____

_____

_____

_____

Day 330 _____ (date)

I am

_____
_____

Today, I will

_____
_____

Today, I

_____
_____

My overall thoughts about my day:

_____
_____
_____
_____
_____

Day 331 _____ (date)

I am

_____

_____

Today, I will

_____

_____

Today, I

_____

_____

My overall thoughts about my day:

_____

_____

_____

_____

_____

Day 332 _____ (date)

I am

_____

_____

Today, I will

_____

_____

Today, I

_____

_____

My overall thoughts about my day:

_____

_____

_____

_____

_____

Day 333 _____ (date)

I am

_____

_____

Today, I will

_____

_____

Today, I

_____

_____

My overall thoughts about my day:

_____

_____

_____

_____

_____

Day 334 _____ (date)

I am

_____

_____

Today, I will

_____

_____

Today, I

_____

_____

My overall thoughts about my day:

_____

_____

_____

_____

_____

BE UNIQUE

Day 335 _____ (date)

I am

_____

_____

Today, I will

_____

_____

Today, I

_____

_____

My overall thoughts about my day:

_____

_____

_____

_____

_____

Day 336 _____ (date)

I am

_____

_____

Today, I will

_____

_____

Today, I

_____

_____

My overall thoughts about my day:

_____

_____

_____

_____

_____

Day 337 _____ (date)

I am

_____

_____

Today, I will

_____

_____

Today, I

_____

_____

My overall thoughts about my day:

_____

_____

_____

_____

_____

Day 338 _____ (date)

I am

_____

_____

Today, I will

_____

_____

Today, I

_____

_____

My overall thoughts about my day:

_____

_____

_____

_____

_____

Day 339 _____ (date)

I am

_____

_____

Today, I will

_____

_____

Today, I

_____

_____

My overall thoughts about my day:

_____

_____

_____

_____

_____

Day 340 _____ (date)

I am

_____

_____

Today, I will

_____

_____

Today, I

_____

_____

My overall thoughts about my day:

_____

_____

_____

_____

_____

339

Be Unique

Day 341 _____ (date)

I am

_____

_____

Today, I will

_____

_____

Today, I

_____

_____

My overall thoughts about my day:

_____

_____

_____

_____

_____

A Journal for Self-Awareness and Self-Acceptance

Day 342 _____ (date)

I am

_____

_____

Today, I will

_____

_____

Today, I

_____

_____

My overall thoughts about my day:

_____

_____

_____

_____

_____

341

BE UNIQUE

Day 343 _____ (date)

I am

_____

_____

Today, I will

_____

_____

Today, I

_____

_____

My overall thoughts about my day:

_____

_____

_____

_____

_____

Day 344 _____ (date)

I am

_____

_____

Today, I will

_____

_____

Today, I

_____

_____

My overall thoughts about my day:

_____

_____

_____

_____

_____

Day 345 _____ (date)

I am

_____

_____

Today, I will

_____

_____

Today, I

_____

_____

My overall thoughts about my day:

_____

_____

_____

_____

_____

Day 346 _____ (date)

I am

_____

_____

Today, I will

_____

_____

Today, I

_____

_____

My overall thoughts about my day:

_____

_____

_____

_____

_____

Day 347 _____ (date)

I am

_____

_____

Today, I will

_____

_____

Today, I

_____

_____

My overall thoughts about my day:

_____

_____

_____

_____

_____

Day 348 _____ (date)

I am

_____

_____

Today, I will

_____

_____

Today, I

_____

_____

My overall thoughts about my day:

_____

_____

_____

_____

BE UNIQUE

Day 349 _____ (date)

I am

_____

_____

Today, I will

_____

_____

Today, I

_____

_____

My overall thoughts about my day:

_____

_____

_____

_____

_____

Day 350 _____ (date)

I am

_____

_____

Today, I will

_____

_____

Today, I

_____

_____

My overall thoughts about my day:

_____

_____

_____

_____

_____

Day 351 _____ (date)

I am

_____

_____

Today, I will

_____

_____

Today, I

_____

_____

My overall thoughts about my day:

_____

_____

_____

_____

_____

Day 352 _____ (date)

I am

_____

_____

Today, I will

_____

_____

Today, I

_____

_____

My overall thoughts about my day:

_____

_____

_____

_____

_____

Day 353 _____ (date)

I am

_____

_____

Today, I will

_____

_____

Today, I

_____

_____

My overall thoughts about my day:

_____

_____

_____

_____

_____

Day 354 _____ (date)

I am

_____

_____

Today, I will

_____

_____

Today, I

_____

_____

My overall thoughts about my day:

_____

_____

_____

_____

_____

Day 355 _____ (date)

I am

_____

_____

Today, I will

_____

_____

Today, I

_____

_____

My overall thoughts about my day:

_____

_____

_____

_____

_____

Day 356 _____ (date)

I am

_____

_____

Today, I will

_____

_____

Today, I

_____

_____

My overall thoughts about my day:

_____

_____

_____

_____

_____

Day 357 _____ (date)

I am

_____

_____

Today, I will

_____

_____

Today, I

_____

_____

My overall thoughts about my day:

_____

_____

_____

_____

_____

Day 358 _____ (date)

I am

_____

_____

Today, I will

_____

_____

Today, I

_____

_____

My overall thoughts about my day:

_____

_____

_____

_____

_____

Day 359 _____ (date)

I am

_____

_____

Today, I will

_____

_____

Today, I

_____

_____

My overall thoughts about my day:

_____

_____

_____

_____

_____

Day 360 _____ (date)

I am

_____

_____

Today, I will

_____

_____

Today, I

_____

_____

My overall thoughts about my day:

_____

_____

_____

_____

_____

Day 361 _____ (date)

I am

_____

_____

Today, I will

_____

_____

Today, I

_____

_____

My overall thoughts about my day:

_____

_____

_____

_____

_____

Day 362_____ (date)

I am

_____

_____

Today, I will

_____

_____

Today, I

_____

_____

My overall thoughts about my day:

_____

_____

_____

_____

_____

Day 363 _____ (date)

I am

_____

_____

Today, I will

_____

_____

Today, I

_____

_____

My overall thoughts about my day:

_____

_____

_____

_____

_____

Day 364 _____ (date)

I am

_____

_____

Today, I will

_____

_____

Today, I

_____

_____

My overall thoughts about my day:

_____

_____

_____

_____

_____

Day 365 _____ (date)

I am

_____

_____

Today, I will

_____

_____

Today, I

_____

_____

My overall thoughts about my day:

_____

_____

_____

_____

_____

CREATING DISTINCTIVE BOOKS
WITH INTENTIONAL RESULTS

We're a collaborative group of creative masterminds
with a mission to produce high-quality books to position
you for monumental success in the marketplace.

Our professional team of writers, editors, designers,
and marketing strategists work closely together to ensure
that every detail of your book is a clear representation
of the message in your writing.

Want to know more?
Write to us at info@publishyourgift.com
or call (888) 949-6228

Discover great books, exclusive offers, and more at
www.PublishYourGift.com

Connect with us on social media

@publishyourgift